COUNTRY PROFILES

HONDURAS

BY GOLRIZ GOLKAR

BELLWETHER MEDIA • MINNEAPOLIS, MN

Blastoff! Discovery launches a new mission: reading to learn. Filled with facts and features, each book offers you an exciting new world to explore!

BLASTOFF! UNIVERSE

BLASTOFF! Beginners — GRADE K

BLASTOFF! READERS — GRADES 1-3

BLASTOFF! DISCOVERY — GRADE 4

This edition first published in 2021 by Bellwether Media, Inc.

No part of this publication may be reproduced in whole or in part without written permission of the publisher.
For information regarding permission, write to Bellwether Media, Inc., Attention: Permissions Department,
6012 Blue Circle Drive, Minnetonka, MN 55343.

Library of Congress Cataloging-in-Publication Data

Names: Golkar, Golriz, author.
Title: Honduras / by Golriz Golkar.
Description: Minneapolis, MN : Bellwether Media, 2021.
  | Series: Blastoff! Discovery: Country Profiles
  | Includes bibliographical references and index.
Audience: Ages 7-13 | Audience: Grades 4-6 | Summary: "Engaging
  images accompany information about Honduras. The combination
  of high-interest subject matter and narrative text is intended for
  students in grades 3 through 8"–Provided by publisher.
Identifiers: LCCN 2020049061 (print) | LCCN 2020049062 (ebook)
  | ISBN 9781644874486 (library binding) | ISBN
  9781648341250 (ebook)
Subjects: LCSH: Honduras–Juvenile literature. | Honduras–Social life
  and customs–Juvenile literature.
Classification: LCC F1503.2 .G65 2021 (print) | LCC F1503.2
  (ebook) | DDC 972.83–dc23
LC record available at https://lccn.loc.gov/2020049061
LC ebook record available at https://lccn.loc.gov/2020049062

Editor: Kieran Downs   Designer: Laura Sowers

Printed in the United States of America, North Mankato, MN.

TABLE OF CONTENTS

LA TIGRA NATIONAL PARK

A family enjoys a hike at La Tigra National Park. As they explore, they spot a waterfall crashing down a mountain. Colorful birds chatter in the lush green forest. A bus then takes them back to Tegucigalpa.

OTHER TOP SITES

CUSUCO NATIONAL PARK

LAKE YOJOA

RÍO PLÁTANO BIOSPHERE RESERVE

SANTA BARBARA FORTRESS

In the city, they eat a **traditional** Honduran lunch at Mercado Los Dolores. Food stalls offer hot *baleadas*. These tortillas stuffed with beans, cheese, and sour cream make a tasty meal. Afterwards, they stroll to the Basílica de Suyapa. This monument honors the **patron saint** of Honduras. They gaze at the magnificent stained-glass windows. Honduras is a country of many wonders!

5

UNDERWATER PARADISE

The Islas de la Bahía are home to colorful coral reefs full of marine life. The reefs are part of the Mesoamerican Barrier Reef, which is the second-largest coral reef in the world.

CARIBBEAN SEA

ISLAS DE LA BAHÍA

GUATEMALA

CHOLOMA

LA CEIBA

SAN PEDRO SULA

HONDURAS

TEGUCIGALPA

EL SALVADOR

NICARAGUA

GULF OF FONSECA

PACIFIC OCEAN

Honduras is located in Central America. It covers 43,278 square miles (112,090 square kilometers). The Caribbean Sea stretches across its northern coast. Guatemala and El Salvador border Honduras to the west and southwest. The Pacific Ocean splashes against Honduras's narrow southern coast in the **Gulf** of Fonseca. Nicaragua lies along the southeastern border.

The capital, Tegucigalpa, is found near the center of Honduras. The country also includes several islands. The three Islas de la Bahía are the largest. They lie north of the **mainland** in the Caribbean Sea.

LANDSCAPE AND CLIMATE

Honduras is mostly mountainous. Mountains and valleys stretch across the west, peaking at Mount Las Minas. Sandy beaches and rolling **plains** cover the northern coastal region. The Ulúa River in the northwest runs north towards the Gulf of Honduras. The **Volcanic** Highlands extend across the southwest region. In the south, the Pacific lowlands center on the Gulf of Fonseca. **Rain forests** cover the eastern Caribbean lowlands, where the Patuca River empties into the sea.

CELAQUE NATIONAL PARK

GULF OF FONSECA

TEGUCIGALPA

Average
seasonal highs
and lows

JANUARY
HIGH: 79 °F (26 °C)
LOW: 59 °F (15 °C)

APRIL
HIGH: 86 °F (30 °C)
LOW: 64 °F (18 °C)

JULY
HIGH: 82 °F (28 °C)
LOW: 65 °F (18 °C)

OCTOBER
HIGH: 80 °F (27 °C)
LOW: 64 °F (18 °C)

°F = degrees Fahrenheit
°C = degrees Celsius

Temperatures in Honduras are warm year-round.
The coasts have a **tropical** climate. Mountain areas
are cooler. The northern coast is rainy. Other regions are
rainy from spring through fall. Winters are usually dry.

WILDLIFE

BROWN-THROATED SLOTH

Honduras is home to many animals. Scarlet macaws, the national bird, soar through the rain forests. There, harpy eagles hunt for brown-throated sloths and spider monkeys in the treetops. Jaguars and coral snakes roam the forest floor as colorful butterflies flutter about. White-tailed deer, the national animal, dash across the plains. Pumas chase after them.

GREEN SEA TURTLE

Fish and crocodiles live along Honduras's coastline. Whale sharks, West Indian manatees, and green sea turtles swim off the Caribbean coast.

CENTRAL AMERICAN CORAL SNAKE

PUMA

HARPY EAGLE

SCARLET MACAW

SCARLET MACAW

Life Span: up to 50 years
Red List Status: least concern

scarlet macaw range = ⬜

LEAST CONCERN	NEAR THREATENED	VULNERABLE	ENDANGERED	CRITICALLY ENDANGERED	EXTINCT IN THE WILD	EXTINCT

More than 9 million people live in Honduras. Around 9 out of 10 Hondurans are *mestizo*, with mixed European and **native** roots. Other **ethnic** groups include native Amerindians. The Lenca people are the most populous Amerindian group in Honduras. Many Hondurans from the West Indies live along the Caribbean coast. The Garifuna people, those with mixed African and Carib Indian **ancestors**, also live in the coastal region.

Many Hondurans are Roman Catholic. A smaller group is Protestant. Spanish is the official language of Honduras. **Dialects** of Amerindian languages are also spoken throughout the country.

FAMOUS FACE

Name: Carlos Campos
Birthday: October 12, 1972
Hometown: El Progreso, Yoro, Honduras
Famous for: Award-winning fashion designer and founder of the first design school in Honduras

SPEAK SPANISH

ENGLISH	SPANISH	HOW TO SAY IT
hello	hola	OH-lah
goodbye	adiós	ah-dee-OHS
please	por favor	pohr fah-VOR
thank you	gracias	grah-SEE-ahs
yes	sí	SEE
no	no	NO

Urban Hondurans live in big cities such as Tegucigalpa and San Pedro Sula. Buses and cars provide transportation. Some people live in cement or brick houses. Poorer Hondurans live in **slums**. Rows of small, crowded rooms called *cuarterías* line the streets.

CHICKEN BUSES

Colorful chicken buses help Hondurans get around. These buses are also used to transport items, including chickens!

Rural Hondurans live in clay or adobe houses in small villages. These people often have less money than urban dwellers. Many of them have no electricity. In these areas, truck owners may give people rides to places.

Hondurans often visit each other on the weekends. Hosts almost always offer their guests drinks or snacks. Guests will often be invited to eat, even if they are unexpected. Hondurans always make sure their guests feel welcome.

Music and dance are at the heart of Honduran **culture**. The Garifuna people made *la punta* music a national favorite. As musicians beat their drums and sing, colorfully dressed dancers shake their hips and pound their feet. The *sique* is a popular folk dance throughout Honduras. People dance in pairs and clap their hands to the lively music.

GARIFUNA DANCER

LEARNING TO READ AND WRITE

Because they have to leave school early, many Hondurans have poor reading and writing skills. Organizations from around the world have been helping Hondurans improve their skills and get good jobs.

Education in Honduras is required and free from first through sixth grade. Students study subjects such as Spanish, math, and science. Many Hondurans leave school to work after sixth grade, especially in rural areas. Most wealthier Hondurans attend high school. They may later attend a trade school or university.

More than half of the Honduran population lives in **poverty**. Many of them are small farmers called *campesinos*. They grow a single crop such as coffee, corn, or beans. Others work on large banana or sugarcane **plantations**. Wealthy Hondurans own land and businesses. Some hold government jobs. Others work in skilled trades.

CAMPESINO

BANANA PLANTATION

SOCCER

Soccer is the most popular sport in Honduras. It is usually played by men and boys. In recent years, girls have begun to play, especially in rural areas. Most villages have a local team that competes on some level. The Honduran national team sometimes plays in World Cup tournaments.

In cities, volleyball and basketball are popular. Wealthy Hondurans may play tennis or golf. Some even enjoy scuba diving. Swimming is another popular water activity. Hondurans also enjoy playing dominoes, cards, and pool. They visit with friends and family in their free time. Church events and movie theaters are popular meeting places.

SCUBA DIVING

HONDURAN JACKS

What You Need:
- 10 large seeds (pumpkin or sunflower seeds work well)
- 1 small stone

Instructions:
1. All players sit on the ground. One player is chosen to start the game.
2. The starting player scatters all the seeds on the ground in front of all the other players.
3. With one hand, the starting player tosses the stone into the air.
4. With the same hand, the starting player must quickly pick up a seed from the ground and keep it in this hand.
5. As the stone falls down, the player must try to catch it in the same hand holding the seed.
6. If the player catches the stone, they move the collected seed to the other hand and try throwing the stone again with the free hand. This player continues until the stone hits the ground before they can collect the next seed.
7. If the stone hits the ground before the player has picked up the next seed, the next player gets a turn. Place any collected seeds on the ground so that the next player has ten.
8. The next round starts after everyone has tried picking up one seed at a time. Players try to pick up one more seed at a time each round.
9. The player who picks up the most seeds without letting the stone touch the ground wins!

HEALTHY FOOD FOR ALL

The World Food Programme has been helping poor Hondurans get access to food. Working with the Honduran government, they ensure that children get to eat healthy food starting at birth.

TORTILLAS

Beans, rice, and corn are Honduran **staples**. Breakfast may include fried beans, corn tortillas, and scrambled eggs. The national dish, *plato típico*, is typically enjoyed at lunch. It contains meat, eggs, beans, avocado, cheese, and tortillas. *Arroz con leche* is a tasty dessert similar to rice pudding. *Topogigios* are sweet, icy summer drinks. They are served in plastic bags.

Pupusas, which are tortillas stuffed with meat, beans, and cheese, are another popular dish. Mashed plantains, spices, and garlic make a northern dish called *machuca*. A seafood and coconut milk soup called *sopa de hombre* is a southern favorite.

PUPUSAS

MACHUCA

HONDURAN ARROZ CON LECHE

This rice pudding makes a tasty dessert or special snack. Have an adult help you make this sweet recipe!

Ingredients:
1 cup medium grain rice
4 cups whole milk
1/2 cup sugar
1/4 cup butter
2 cinnamon sticks
1 lemon peel
Cinnamon powder

Steps:

1. Wash the rice and drain it well.

2. Place the milk, sugar, lemon peel, and cinnamon sticks in a saucepan and cook together over high heat.

3. When the milk begins to boil, stir in the rice and reduce heat to the lowest setting.

4. Let the pudding cook for about an hour, then remove from the stove.

5. Remove the lemon peel and cinnamon sticks from the rice.

6. Mix in the butter until it is well absorbed. Let the pudding cool.

7. Serve in small bowls and sprinkle with cinnamon.

Most Hondurans celebrate Christian holidays. During Holy Week before Easter, Hondurans attend church and may skip eating meat. Once a year, each Honduran community celebrates its patron saint. The largest patron saint celebration in Honduras is the La Ceiba Carnival in May. It attracts thousands of visitors. Colorfully dressed locals choose a Carnival queen and celebrate with music, dance, and parades in the street.

HOLY WEEK

KIDS RULE!

September 10 is Children's Day. Honduran children are given gifts and sweets.

CHILDREN'S DAY

For Christmas, Hondurans decorate their homes and have parties. Families enjoy traditional meals and exchange presents. No matter the time of year, Hondurans celebrate their family and **heritage**!

1823
Honduras joins the United Provinces of Central America and gains independence from Mexico

1502
Christopher Columbus arrives in Honduras and gives the country its name

1969
Honduras fights a brief war with El Salvador over immigration

1539
The Spanish conquer the native people of Honduras

1838
Honduras becomes an independent republic

1821
Honduras wins independence from Spain and becomes part of Mexico

1998
Hurricane Mitch hits Honduras, leaving millions homeless

2016
A four-year international mission targeted at tackling Honduran corruption begins

1981
Roberto Suazo Cordova is elected president, going on to lead the first civilian government in over a century

2012
The Mara Salvatrucha and Mara Dieciocho street gangs declare a truce to end ongoing violence

HONDURAS FACTS

Official Name: Republic of Honduras

Flag of Honduras: The Honduran flag has three equal horizontal bands. The top and bottom blue bands represent the Pacific Ocean and the Caribbean Sea. The middle white band represents the land of Honduras as well as the peace and wealth of Hondurans. Five blue stars are centered on the white band in an X pattern. These represent the members of the former Federal Republic of Central America.

Area: 43,278 square miles
(112,090 square kilometers)

Capital City: Tegucigalpa

Important Cities: San Pedro Sula, Choloma, La Ceiba

Population:
9,235,340 (July 2020)

WHERE PEOPLE LIVE

COUNTRYSIDE
41.6%

CITY
58.4%

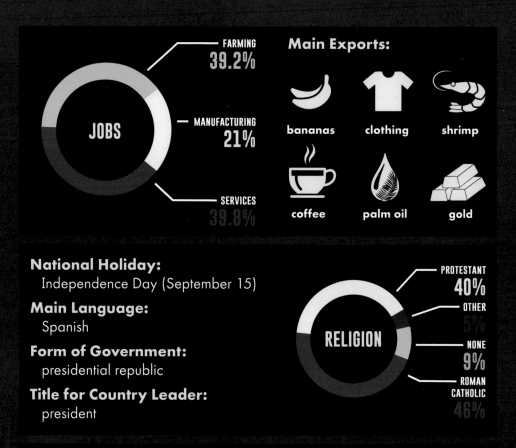

FARMING
39.2%

JOBS

MANUFACTURING
21%

SERVICES
39.8%

Main Exports:

bananas

clothing

shrimp

coffee

palm oil

gold

National Holiday:
Independence Day (September 15)

Main Language:
Spanish

Form of Government:
presidential republic

Title for Country Leader:
president

RELIGION

PROTESTANT
40%

OTHER
5%

NONE
9%

ROMAN CATHOLIC
46%

Unit of Money:
lempira

GLOSSARY

ancestors—relatives who lived long ago

culture—the beliefs, arts, and ways of life in a place or society

dialects—local ways of speaking particular languages

ethnic—related to a group of people who share customs and an identity

gulf—part of an ocean or sea that extends into land

heritage—the traditions, achievements, and beliefs that are part of the history of a group of people

mainland—a continent or main part of a continent

native—originally from the area or related to a group of people that began in the area

patron saint—a saint who is believed to look after a country or group of people

plains—large areas of flat land

plantations—large farms that grow coffee beans, cotton, rubber, or other crops; plantations are mainly found in warm climates.

poverty—the state of lacking money or possessions

rain forests—thick green forests that receive a lot of rain

rural—related to the countryside

slums—parts of cities that are crowded or have poor housing

staples—widely used foods or other items

traditional—related to customs, ideas, or beliefs handed down from one generation to the next

tropical—part of the tropics; the tropics is a hot, rainy region near the equator

urban—related to cities and city life

volcanic—related to a hole in the earth called a volcano; when a volcano erupts, hot ash, gas, or melted rock called lava shoots out.

TO LEARN MORE

AT THE LIBRARY

Bowman, Chris. *El Salvador*. Minneapolis, Minn.: Bellwether Media, 2020.

Green, Sara. *Ancient Maya*. Minneapolis, Minn.: Bellwether Media, 2020.

Wehner, Lauren, Leta McGaffey, and Michael Spilling. *Honduras*. New York, N.Y.: Cavendish Square, 2019.

ON THE WEB

FACTSURFER

Factsurfer.com gives you a safe, fun way to find more information.

1. Go to www.factsurfer.com.

2. Enter "Honduras" into the search box and click Q.

3. Select your book cover to see a list of related content.

INDEX

The images in this book are reproduced through the courtesy of: dstephens, cover; Carlos Torres, pp. 4-5; Andrew M. Snyder/ Getty Images, p. 5 (Cusuco National Park); Jpiks, p. 5 (Lake Yojoa); mauritius images GmbH/ Alamy, p. 5 (Río Plátano Biosphere Reserve); mundosemfim, pp. 5 (Santa Barbara Fortress), 21 (top); Christian Kober 1/ Alamy Stock Photo, p. 8; Juan Carlos/ Alamy Stock Photo, pp. 9, 22; Manuel Chinchilla, p. 9 (Tegucigalpa); Volodymyr Burdiak, p. 10 (puma); Lukas Kovarik, p. 10 (brown-throated sloth); Rich Carey, p. 10 (green sea turtle); Ferdy Timmerman, p. 10 (Central American coral snake); Marcus VDT, p. 10 (harpy eagle); David Havel, pp. 10-11; Jodi Jacobson, p. 12; WENN Rights Ltd/ Alamy Stock Photo, p. 13 (top); milosk50, p. 13 (bottom); Lozzy Squire/ Alamy Stock Photo, p. 14; Omri Eliyahu, p. 15; Keith Levit / Alamy Stock Photo, p. 16; Devon Stephens / Alamy Stock Photo, p. 17; Charles O. Cecil/ Alamy Stock Photo, p. 18; Marco Vasquez, p. 19 (top); Image Professionals GmbH/ Alamy Stock Photo, p. 19 (bottom); mooinblack, p. 20; chittakorn59, p. 21 (bottom); AS Food studio, p. 23 (pupusas); Clara Gonzalez, p. 23 (machuca); Zuzana Suz, p. 23 (arroz con leche); 615 collection/ Alamy Stock Photo, p. 24; REUTERS/ Alamy Stock Photo, p. 25; Everett Collection, p. 26; Robert_Ford, p. 27; Dirick Halstead/ Getty Images, p. 27 (bottom); Oleg_Mit, p. 29 (banknote); Yaroslaff, p. 29 (coin).